Original title:
Pansy Pages

Copyright © 2025 Creative Arts Management OÜ
All rights reserved.

Author: Zachary Prescott
ISBN HARDBACK: 978-1-80566-781-0
ISBN PAPERBACK: 978-1-80566-801-5

A Kaleidoscope of Mirth

In gardens where the giggles bloom,
Colors dance and chase away gloom.
Butterflies in bowties prance,
While flowers join the silly dance.

Bumblebees wear tiny hats,
Buzzing round like chatty cats.
Each petal sports a playful grin,
As laughter spills like sunlight in.

Garden of Forgotten Verses

In corners where the rhymes forgot,
We find a line that's quite the plot.
A sunflower winks with a smile,
While daisies gossip for a while.

Crickets chirp a jolly tune,
Underneath the balmy moon.
Each word blooms and then decays,
In this garden of silly ways.

Tattered Leaves of Spring

The leaves sing songs with raspy cheer,
As breezes whisper – no one's near.
A crow wears spectacles, looks wise,
While squirrels skip with springtime sighs.

Worn-out petals tell a joke,
About the tree that loves to poke.
Nature laughs as seasons grin,
In this world where fun begins.

The Secret Languages of Flora

Amidst the blooms, secrets unfold,
In whispers shared and laughter bold.
Dandelions draft the town's best news,
While violets wear the brightest shoes.

Petal gossip travels fast,
As roots conspire, snickers cast.
In the chatter of the breeze,
The flora giggles with such ease.

Beneath the Blossom's Veil

Beneath the veil of blossoms bright,
A bumblebee took flight in fright.
He buzzed so loud, a clumsy dance,
I laughed so hard, lost in a trance.

The petals whispered silly tales,
Of ants in shorts and windy gales.
A caterpillar wore a hat,
Chasing a snail that looked like that!

The flowers giggled in the breeze,
Spilling secrets with such ease.
A flower pot with legs ran past,
I chased it down, it was a blast!

Oh, carefree days in garden's hold,
With every bloom, a story told.
In laughter's grasp, we play and sway,
Beneath the veil of blooms so gay.

Where Gardens Dream

Where laughter grows and zinnias chat,
A squirrel just stole a gardener's hat.
The roses giggle, full of cheer,
As daisies dance, they bring us near.

In tulip lands, where dreams unfold,
A ladybug tells the best of gold.
With clouds of candy, all the crew,
The sun drips syrup, fun ensues!

Between the rows of greens and reds,
The gnomes all joke while lying in beds.
A sunflower does a wiggly twirl,
Chasing its shadows, giving a whirl.

At dusk, the stars join in the fun,
Each speck a wink, a cheeky pun.
Where gardens dream and laughter beams,
A whimsical world where nonsense gleams.

Sunlit Thoughts

In sunlit thoughts, the daisies laugh,
They take a break, then draw a graph.
A squirrel plots a daring heist,
For acorns galore, he rolls the dice!

The sunbeam tickles a tulip's head,
While mischief whispers, "Get out of bed!"
A dandelion with glasses near,
Reads funny books, and spreads good cheer.

A butterfly recites a riddle,
To corral the ants, who giggle and fiddle.
A wind that brings marshmallow fluff,
Tugging all petals, it's such good stuff!

Oh, basking in playful delight,
Where thoughts of sun cast shadows bright,
In fields of joy, embrace the day,
With sunlit thoughts in gentle sway.

The Language of Petals

The language of petals is quite the sight,
They scribble secrets in pure delight.
A bloom tells jokes to the bumblebee,
Crafting a joke as sweet as can be.

With every flutter and gentle sway,
They gossip softly in spring's ballet.
A rose once boasted of its grand style,
While violets shrugged, "It's just our wile!"

The marigold hums a silly tune,
While chubby bees dance, twirling in June.
A bold sunflower wears shades so bright,
Claiming it's cooler than day turns to night.

In this garden where laughter reigns,
Each petal's giggle unchains the gains.
The world's a stage where blooms convey,
A symphony comical, every day.

Underneath the Petal Canopy

Beneath the blooms, the insects dance,
A ladybug takes a chance.
With tiny boots that squeak and slide,
They trip on petals, full of pride.

A butterfly wearing striped pajamas,
Stretches out like a field of dramas.
While bees buzz around on coffee breaks,
In search of sweet treats, like silly flakes.

Diary of a Flowering Heart

Dear diary, today I bloomed,
But oh dear, I nearly doomed.
A gardener's hoe came whistling by,
I ducked so fast, I reached the sky!

With every breeze, I sway and grin,
The sun laughed hard, I felt like kin.
The petals giggle in the light,
As bees tell jokes that take their flight.

The Scribbles of Nature

On a leaf, I found a sketch,
A worm had drawn, oh what a fetch!
It twirled and swirled in wiggly lines,
While ants critiqued with tiny signs.

A flower cried, "I'm deeply touched!"
As petals fluttered much and clutched.
The wind, it laughed, "You're all so sweet!"
Then tripped on roots, fell at my feet!

Floral Echoes

In the garden, giggles rise,
When daisies talk with open eyes.
A tulip whispers to a rose,
"Your perfume's stronger, maybe pose?"

The sunlight beams in playful jest,
As shadows play their little quest.
They leap and bound, all in a line,
Across the blooms, it's truly fine!

Soliloquy of the Quiet Garden

In the garden, whispers play,
Petals gossip through the day.
Bumblebees in bowler hats,
Munching crumbs with friendly chats.

Worms are writing their memoirs,
Underneath the blooming stars.
Squirrels juggling acorn snacks,
Plotting mischief with sly quacks.

Rain decides to join the fun,
Splashing puddles, everyone!
Mice with shoes and tiny ties,
Dance beneath the grayish skies.

Garden gnomes with painted grins,
Keeping watch as laughter spins.
In this world, all things conspire,
To make the mundane, something higher.

Legacies of the Living Blooms

Flowers boast of tales untold,
Waving hands, both brave and bold.
Daisies sneer at tulip flair,
While daisies try a daring hair.

Sunflowers take a selfie now,
Holding blooms with furrowed brow.
Lilies laugh at their own scent,
Making sure their time is spent.

Violets gossip day and night,
Ducking when a breeze takes flight.
Petunias prance in polka dots,
Trading secrets from their pots.

Rose bushes wear their thorns with pride,
While irises just roll their eyes.
Lively flora keeps the peace,
In a world where joy won't cease.

The Iridescent Stanza

In the sunlight, colors gleam,
Each petal has a secret dream.
Chasing rainbows on a whim,
Every bloom, a playful hymn.

Butterflies with silly face,
Flutter in a crazy race.
With a twirl and a lost shoe,
They giggle in the morning dew.

Tulips shiver from the tease,
Waving 'hi' to passing bees.
Laughter wafts like summer breeze,
Easing into joyful ease.

Amidst the fun, the garden sways,
In a dance of bright displays.
Colors burst, a wild scene,
In this place, where smiles convene.

Ink Dripped Petals

Writing stories in the air,
Petals dripping, oh so rare.
Ink and laughter twine and spin,
As the garden loves to grin.

Dandelions boast their art,
Pages turning, what a start!
Bees with quills and paper stacks,
Scribble jokes behind their backs.

Every bloom a page anew,
Tales of mishaps, silly too.
Vases filled with giggles bright,
Wink at passing day and night.

Secret plots beneath the leaves,
Ticklish tales the garden weaves.
In this scripted, bloom-filled place,
Ink drips laughter, love, and grace.

Embracing Nature's Ink

In the garden where giggles bloom,
Ladybugs dance, dispelling gloom.
Petals whisper secrets, oh so sly,
To the bumblebee buzzing by.

Worms write letters in squiggly script,
Hiding from raindrops, quite well-equipped.
Sunflowers chuckle with faces so bright,
As butterflies twirl in pure delight.

The Garden's Subtle Confessions

Tulips gossip near the fence,
Sharing tales of missed romance.
The daisies giggle at the ants,
While shadows play their little prance.

A dandelion puffs, a shy retreat,
Wishing for moments oh so sweet.
Frogs croak laughs, in croaky tones,
As the moonlight wraps them in soft loans.

Inked Gardens, Untold Stories

Petals prance like actors on stage,
Crafting tales from nature's page.
Vines write verses in the air,
And snails compose without a care.

The sun winks and the shadows play,
As beetles host a grand ballet.
Each leaf a laugh, each stalk a smile,
Nature's humor stretches a mile.

Requiem for the Torn Petal

Once a bright star with colors bold,
Now just a whisper, a tale retold.
A gust of wind swept through one day,
Leaving a story in disarray.

The rose weeps for its fluttered friend,
While bees buzz low, their songs extend.
But even torn, there's beauty still,
In laughter shared and nature's thrill.

The Blooming Chronicle

In the garden, pranks unfold,
Flowers giggle, stories told.
Bees wear shades, a sunny flair,
Butterflies dance without a care.

Tulips trip on the grass so green,
Roses blush, a comedic scene.
Dandelions puff, they aim to tease,
While violets wink with cheeky ease.

A daffodil slips, oh what a sight!
Laughter echoes from left to right.
Each petal plays a jolly tune,
Under the watch of the lazy moon.

In this patch, no frown may stay,
Nature's jesters come out to play.
With every bloom, a wave of cheer,
In this garden, laughter's near.

Sighs of the Garden Goddess

A flower sighed, too bright a day,
"Why always bloom? Can I just play?"
The sun grinned wide, a playful tease,
"Shine, dear petal, with effortless ease."

Tulip in a hat, oh what a style,
"Look at me; I'm such a file!"
Daisy struggled to stay upright,
Comically wobbling left and right.

The lilies laughed, hiding behind,
"Come bloom with us; you're one of a kind!"
Lilac chuckled, "A joke's in bloom,
Let's plot some fun, dispel the gloom!"

The goddess shook her head with glee,
Her garden's jesters, wild and free.
In every sigh, the laughter grows,
Among the petals, joy overflows.

Whispers of Color

Colors chatter in vibrant hues,
"Who wore it best? Let's play the blues!"
The yellow daisy called to red,
"Let's debate on what's best to spread!"

Bluebells giggled, tipsy and bright,
In a dance-off under the light.
"Watch me twirl!" said the cheeky green,
While orange snickered, "I reign supreme!"

Every bloom had something to say,
Spilling secrets in a playful way.
An accidental splash, uh-oh, a mess,
But their hues just laughed, feeling blessed.

Whispers of color filled the air,
"Join our party, if you dare!"
In this world where hues take flight,
A canvas of laughter, pure delight!

The Language of Blooming Hearts

Petals whisper, hearts take flight,
"Do you see that? What a sight!"
The roses wink with a playful pout,
While sunflowers turn, chuckling out loud.

"Why so blue?" a hyacinth cried,
"Join the fun, come take a ride!"
The marigold grinned, "Try my cheer,
In the dance of petals, no room for fear!"

A daffodil jokes, with a pun so bright,
"Who needs the sun when you have delight?"
Every heart in bloom, a tale unique,
Laughter's the language, not just a peak.

With each petal, the banter flows,
In a garden where humor grows.
The language of blooms, so light and sweet,
Builds a chorus, a rhythm, a beat.

Gentle Hues of Spring

In gardens bright, the colors play,
Where flowers laugh and dance away.
The daisies make a silly face,
While tulips try to keep their place.

With every breeze, the blooms conspire,
To tickle noses, spark desire.
A bee buzzes by, a jester's tune,
As petals wink beneath the moon.

The violets giggle, the roses grin,
As butterflies swirl, spinning in.
They tease the blooms, a playful shout,
In springtime's joy, there's no room for doubt.

So let us cheer these funny scenes,
Where blossoms nurture blissful dreams.
In hues so gentle, laughter flows,
In this bouquet where humor grows.

Whispered Blooms

In secret corners flowers murmur,
As daisies play games and giggle, a slumber.
Roses wink with petals blush,
Each telling tales in a colorful hush.

The laughter spreads from bud to bud,
As butterflies dance on a whimsy flood.
They jest with bees about lost socks,
While pansies plot around the clocks.

A dandelion shouts, "Look at me!"
While petals trip over glee.
Tulips wear hats made of dew,
In this garden, the fun's never through.

So join the blooms and share their cheer,
In whispered jokes only they hear.
A colorful scene, so merry and bright,
In this flowery world, pure delight.

Petals on the Wind

Petals flutter like dancers bold,
Spinning stories that never get old.
With each gust, they twist and twirl,
Making the whole garden swirl.

A sunflower shouts, "Catch that breeze!"
While wind whispers tales to the trees.
The roses giggle, a ticklish sight,
As they sway under soft moonlight.

The snapdragons snicker, a cheeky grin,
While pansies plot where fun begins.
A petal lands on a puppy's nose,
And laughter erupts, as humor grows.

So chase the petals, let spirits soar,
In laughter's grip, who could ask for more?
With colors flying on spring's delight,
Each flutter a giggle, pure and bright.

Kaleidoscope of Color

A splash of hues, a funny show,
As blooms collide in colorful flow.
The marigolds dance with zest and flair,
While zinnias giggle without a care.

In splendid chaos, colors clash,
As the daisies and violets make a splash.
They tease the tulips, a bright parade,
In this garden where fun's displayed.

Each petal holds a joke to share,
A whimsical carpet, beyond compare.
With every bloom, a chuckle grows,
In this kaleidoscope where laughter flows.

So come enjoy this vivid spree,
Where every flower holds a key.
To giggles and grins, all on display,
In a garden of joy, where colors play.

Fragments of a Garden Tale

In a garden of laughs, where daisies speak,
A tulip winks slyly, but the roses are meek.
A gopher wears glasses, claims he's a sage,
While squirrels juggle nuts on the old wooden stage.

With chattering fairies on petals so bright,
They flutter and flitter, a comical sight.
The daisies keep gossiping, oh what a fuss,
As the sun slinks away, and the moon joins the bus.

Bumblebees buzzing with jokes in their flight,
While laughing leaves rustle, creating delight.
The hedgehog makes tea, but it's brewed with a twist,
With each sip we chuckle, "What's that on the list?"

So come to this garden, where silliness grows,
With laughter as blossoms, and joy that just flows.
A world of hilarity, where whimsy will reign,
In the fragments of tales, we'll dance in the rain.

Echoes of Flora

In a meadow of whispers, the flowers convene,
"Did you hear about Daisy?" she slipped on some green.
Sunflowers laugh loud from their tall, lofty thrones,
While wind carries chuckles in soft, leafy tones.

The violets gossip, "Oh, what a display!
Did you see that old snail? It danced all the way!"
Petunias sprinkle humor with each sunny hue,
As the daisies declare, "We'll throw a grand do!"

A butterfly stumbles, caught in a breeze,
Its dance is a tumble, with grace it just flees.
The bees buzz a tune, oh what a delight,
In this floral serenade, from day into night.

With laughter that echoes through each dewy petal,
The garden's alive, like a loping foxtrot medal.
In the echoes of flora, the fun never wanes,
With smiles blooming wide, washing away all strains.

Unfolding Secrets

Behind every bloom, there's a tale to unfold,
About daisies who whisper, and secrets they hold.
The garden's a mansion, with flora galore,
Where secrets get spilled, and we all just implore.

Beneath leafy arches, a squirrel's on trial,
For stealing the acorns, now sitting in style.
With daisies as lawyers, and tulips as clerks,
The laughter erupts, oh what comical quirks!

A garden gnome grins, with mischief in eyes,
As the flowers keep plotting undercover surprise.
A scheme to outshine the moon with their glow,
And who would have thought, such talent would show?

So let's share this humor, beneath the sun's rays,
As blooms dance in laughter, and sway in their plays.
In the secrets unfolding, where fun takes its claim,
The garden turns vibrant, and brightens the game.

Tapestry of Tenderness

In a tapestry woven with laughter and cheer,
The garden's a canvas where joy rears its ear.
Petals dive into giggles, and roots form a band,
While flowers play pranks, isn't nature just grand?

A rose with a tickle, it pokes at a bee,
The commotion that follows is quite a sight to see.
With tulips breaking into spontaneous dance,
The giggles keep growing, oh what a chance!

The daisies are activists, rallying at dawn,
"Let's dance 'til the dew and the daylight are gone!"
The sun sneaks a smile, while the clouds roll with glee,
As the breeze carries whispers of pure jubilee.

In this joyful garden, so vivid, so bright,
Where love is a laughter, and laughter ignites.
We craft a sweet tapestry, stitched with pure fun,
Under skies woven gently, till the day is done.

Ephemeral Ink

In a world of scribbles, we dance and twirl,
A jumbled mess, oh what a whirl!
With ink that smudges, we giggle with glee,
A quirky tale, just you and me.

Doodle bugs fly on their paper planes,
Chasing after words like runaway trains.
Each stroke a giggle, each dot a grin,
This laughter of lines, let the fun begin!

Oh what a joy, this ephemeral art,
Drawn by the chaos of a dreaming heart.
With puddles of colors that gently spill,
We laugh at the mess, oh what a thrill!

So take a pen, let your spirit flow,
In this silly world, let's put on a show.
With joyous scribbles, let freedom sink,
In our laughter, we find ephemeral ink.

Colors of the Serene

In a garden of hues that shimmer and gleam,
Colors collide like a daydream's beam.
With laughter like petals, they dance in the sun,
Each shade a tickle, a giggly fun run.

Swirls of pink giggles and blue chuckles roam,
A jester's parade, where these colors call home.
Yellow like sunshine, and green like the grass,
Together they frolic, in this merry class.

With splashes of orange that bounce with delight,
They spin in a whirlwind, a colorful flight.
Sipping on raindrops, they swirl and play,
Painting the world in the funniest way!

So let the palette bring smiles to the air,
In every bright corner, a reason to care.
With laughter and colors, we're free to be seen,
In this whimsical world of the colors serene!

Pageant of the Blossoms

A festival blooms in the laughter-filled breeze,
Blossoms in costumes, oh what a tease!
With petals for skirts and leaves like a hat,
Each flower a dancer, and oh could they chat!

In this grand pageant, the daisies take flight,
With tulips in sequins, all giggly and bright.
The roses will twirl, in a delicate spin,
While poppies chuckle, and join in the din.

A parade of scents and vibrant displays,
In laughter's embrace, they twirl through their days.
They whisper sweet secrets, as roots intertwine,
This pageant of blossoms, so funny, divine!

So let's raise a toast to this floral delight,
With humor and joy that will lift spirits bright.
In this riot of colors, let laughter be tossed,
In a pageant of blooms, we'll never be lost!

The Essence of Springtime

In the essence of spring, the jokes come alive,
Bouncing like bunnies, where giggles survive.
The grass tickles toes, oh what a delight,
As flowers gossip beneath the moonlight.

The sun wears a grin with its golden face,
While clouds play hide and seek, a cozy embrace.
With buds full of laughter, the trees start to sway,
In the essence of spring, we all come to play.

Each raindrop a chuckle, each breeze a good jest,
Nature's own humor, we're feeling so blessed.
With blooms all around, and laughter in tow,
In springtime's embrace, we let the joy flow.

So welcome the season with arms open wide,
In the essence of spring, let's enjoy the ride.
For every sweet moment, a giggle we'll find,
In spring's funny heartbeat, we're blissfully kind!

The Story in Each Bloom

In gardens where giggles grow,
Petals dance to a funny show.
Each bloom with a tale to tell,
Of bees that bumble and rings of a bell.

With colors that brighten the day,
They jive and wiggle in their own way.
A daisy shares jokes, a rose tells a pun,
Together they laugh, oh what fun!

In the sun's warm embrace they reside,
Gambling with clouds, the breeze as their guide.
Tulips trumpet their silly delight,
While violets chuckle, 'Isn't this bright?'

Nature's comedians, blooming in rhyme,
Sharing their antics in summertime.
So when you wander where laughter flows,
Remember each bloom wears a hat of prose.

Petals Whispering Secrets

Under the moon's glimmering gaze,
Petals gossip in playful ways.
They spill the tea on the blooming crowd,
With twists and turns, all bright and loud.

Forget the drama of city streets,
Nature's chatters bring delightful feats.
The tulips tease with a winking eye,
While daisies giggle as they sigh.

"So and so went blooming bright!"
A sunflower claims with pure delight.
"Did you hear what that lilac said?
It's all about who gets to the bed!"

In joyful whispers, they share their days,
While marigolds burst with sunlit rays.
A secret club of colorful blooms,
Laughter unfurls and joy resumes.

Flora's Literary Embrace

In a library made of vines,
Plants gather for tea and funny lines.
A sunflower reads, a daisy takes note,
While roses debate the best love quote.

Their stories are wild as butterflies fly,
With humor wrapping like clouds in the sky.
"Who wrote this one? It's downright absurd!"
As thorns punctuate humor with every word.

A bookworm worm twists through the grass,
Critiquing the prose as he happens to pass.
"Oh dear, more drama in this old tome!"
While ivy giggles, "Get back to your home!"

Flora's embrace is a wordplay delight,
As petals spin tales under stars bright.
Each chapter a prank, each line a jest,
In this botanical world, they laugh with zest.

Soul of the Blossom

In the heart of each blossom's wink,
Lies a spirit that loves to think.
With joy in their veins, they sprout and sway,
Tickling the air in a playful way.

A petal's soul may long to sing,
In the dance of life, they joyfully swing.
They wear coconuts, they wear hats,
Engaging in silly chats with the chats!

"Do you believe in garden gnomes?"
A tulip guffaws, "They're our garden homes!"
Each stem a comic with tricks to share,
In floral gatherings, laughter fills the air.

So next time you pause near blooms so bright,
Listen closely, you might find delight.
For in every petal, a spirit lies,
With jokes and laughter that touch the skies.

Chronicles of the Flourishing

In a garden where gnomes dance,
And tulips sport a fine romance,
Petunias giggle, daffodils play,
The bees buzz in a humor-filled way.

Daisies wear their sunny hats,
While butterflies do acrobats,
Worms sing ballads underground,
As laughter blooms all around.

With floppy ears, a rabbit leaps,
In rainbow hues, the garden keeps,
A secret party under the moon,
Where flowers break into a tune.

So here's to blooms and merry scents,
Where nature pulls its funny hints,
In this kooky floral spree,
Every petal's full of glee!

Versions of the Violet Breeze

The wind whispers jokes through the trees,
Bringing chuckles on the soft breeze,
Petals tumble with a silly sway,
As they giggle in their own ballet.

Lavenders laugh in purple tones,
Tickling the air with crafty drones,
Forget-me-nots wink, so sincere,
"Don't leave us, we're always near!"

A pansy, bold, wears a goofy grin,
Cracking jokes, it pulls you in,
"So stop and smell us," they declare,
"With humor wrapped in scented air!"

In this garden of whimsy divine,
The flowers tell tales, intertwine,
Every breeze a silly tease,
As colors dance with perfect ease.

Ode to the Hidden Garden

Behind the fence, a giggly tale,
With roses donned in a bright veil,
They plot mischief, make up schemes,
In this realm of colorful dreams.

A sunflower with a cheeky grin,
Whispers secrets, lets fun begin,
Vines weave stories, twist and twine,
As laughter flows like sweet red wine.

The peeking daisies wave hello,
They play hopscotch in a row,
With every breeze, they crack a smile,
In this quirky garden aisle.

So join the joy, embrace the cheer,
In this hidden realm, draw near,
Where every bloom is part of the jest,
And every petal knows how to fest!

Tales from the Petal Path

On the petal path, laughter roams,
With whimsical whispers and happy gnomes,
The flowers dance in quirky pairs,
Telling tales through the fragrant airs.

Calendulas sing, crooning bright,
While violets giggle, taking flight,
A jasmine's prank leaves all in shock,
As daisies jump on a ticking clock.

The breeze carries tales of delight,
Of a rose who planned a silly fight,
With tulips trading witty jabs,
Creating moments to make you grab.

So stroll along this cheer-filled track,
Where every bloom thinks it's a knack,
To bring some joy, a chuckle or two,
On the petal path, we welcome you!

Lush Reveries

In the garden where giggles bloom,
A butterfly flits, dispelling gloom.
Daisies gossip in the morning dew,
As bees wear hats of sticky glue.

Sunshine spills like lemonade,
While rabbits plot a fresh parade.
Their little tails wiggle with glee,
A sight that's funnier than a tree!

The flowers dance in silly shoes,
And sneaky ants spread ridiculous news.
They tiptoe past a snoozy snail,
Who dreams of tales on a sailboat trail.

Laughter bubbles through the air,
As birds swap jokes without a care.
In this whimsical space we dwell,
Where laughter rings like a magic bell.

Inked with Aroma

With canvases of scents so bright,
The baker's dog sniffs day and night.
Cupcakes float through the puffy air,
As sprinkles dance without a care.

A jar of jam begins to sing,
While a donut wears a chocolate ring.
Jelly beans plot a great escape,
In a race with a yellow grape.

The jammy painters giggle loud,
As sunshine brushes through the crowd.
Colors swirl in a wacky mix,
Creating stories and silly tricks.

The aroma of fun makes us swoon,
As gummy bears tap dance under the moon.
In this land where flavors rhyme,
We toast to tartness, sublime!

The Palette of Memories

Brushstrokes of laughter fill the room,
A pie sits waiting, covered in bloom.
Old tales of cats with hats so tall,
Echo in giggles that bounce off the wall.

Rainbow noodles twist and twirl,
As silly stories begin to unfurl.
A jester's cap atop a spoon,
Makes even broccoli burst into tune!

Paint splatters dance in happy delight,
As macaroni moons glow through the night.
In the crock of creativity, we play,
Where munching and chuckling fill our day.

Memories blend like colors bright,
Each laughter a spark, igniting the night.
In this vibrant world, we feast with glee,
Crafting our joy, wild and free!

Chasing the Colors

Chasing colors on a midsummer breeze,
Silly squirrels wear party hats with ease.
A polka-dotted frog leaps with flair,
While a slow snail snaps a selfie with care.

Wandering through the playful hue,
A rainbow trots, we giggle anew.
Candy clouds float in the sky,
As gummy bears giggle and give a sigh.

A playful palette paints the day,
With swirls of mischief in every way.
From the contrasts of sweet and sour,
To the vibrant bursts of a joke's power.

We chase the colors, we dance and pretend,
In our funny realm, there's no need to mend.
Every moment's a brush in the air,
Creating a canvas of laughter to share.

Veils of Violet Stories

In a garden where secrets giggle,
Petals dance and flowers wiggle.
Bees buzz jokes, oh what a scene,
While butterflies wear crowns of green.

A daisy whispers to a rose,
"You're too prissy, everyone knows!"
The tulips chuckle, bright and loud,
As the sun takes a silly bow, so proud.

With every bloom, a tale unfolds,
Of cheeky critters, brash and bold.
A garden party, laughter flows,
With the silliest of garden prose.

So come, spread joy with every petal,
Life's a joke, a merry medal.
In this patch of vibrant hues,
Laughter lingers on every muse.

Colored Chronicles of the Garden

In the patch where colors clash,
A playful gnome waits for a splash.
He wears a hat of lemon gleam,
And dances like he's in a dream.

The carrots gossip, roots entwine,
"This cabbage thinks it's so divine!"
With squinty eyes, they all agree,
These veggies are a sight to see!

Underneath the sun's warm rays,
Grasshoppers sing in funny ways.
Each hop a pun, each chirp a jest,
A garden feast of laugh-filled fest!

So grab a spade, let's dig for fun,
In this colorful, silly run.
With hearts so light, and spirits high,
We'll dance beneath the painted sky.

Heart of the Botanical

In gardens grand where flowers chat,
They gossip loud, just like the cat.
Bees buzzing with a silly tune,
Promising nectar 'neath the moon.

The daisies dance, with heads held high,
While ivy curls, trying to fly.
A tulip trips, falls on its face,
It laughs, and bounces back with grace.

Fluffy clouds join in for the fun,
Creating shadows, a game begun.
Sunflowers grin, they've got the sway,
In this floral ruckus, all is play.

So here's to blooms with jolly cheer,
Who smile at life with nary a fear.
In this leafy world, so vast and wide,
The heart of plants beats with a laugh inside.

Blooming Whispers

Whispers float on petals soft,
Like secrets shared from loft to loft.
A dandelion tips its hat,
To passing winds, how about that?

Cacti giggle, poking fun,
While daffodils bask in the sun.
'Don't touch me!' shouts the purple thorn,
'I've learned my lesson, I've been worn!'

The violets play a card game rare,
Shuffling leaves with utmost care.
Laughter echoes through the dew,
In this garden, it's all brand new!

Every bloom shares tales untold,
Of summer's warmth and winter's cold.
Let's gather round, the jokes will sprout,
In the realm of flowers, there's never doubt.

Chronicles of Petal Dreams

In the night, petals dream and boast,
About the sun they love the most.
They spin tales of perfume and grace,
Finding joy in every space.

Petunias cracking jokes all day,
While marigolds join in the play.
A rose slips, falls flat on its nose,
And laughs aloud, as flowers do those.

Tales of bees, their silly flights,
Whirling and twirling like small kites.
A sunflower sings a funny rhyme,
Of bees who dance in perfect time.

The petals cheer, their dreams collide,
With every laugh, they swell with pride.
So gather close for this floral scene,
Where dreams delight and laughter's keen.

A Symphony of Silenced Blooms

In the hush of twilight, blooms conspire,
Crafting tunes like a secret choir.
They sway and shuffle, try to fit,
In a world that loves to laugh a bit.

A geranium with a witty quip,
Tells a joke, gives petals a flip.
'Why did the leaf fall from its tree?'
'Because it wanted to fly free!'

Orchids nod with sophisticated grace,
While pansies paint smiles on every face.
Even the fungi join in the mix,
Adding flavors, a palette of tricks.

So let's applaud this leafy band,
For each bloom lends a helping hand.
In perfect synch, the laughter swells,
In the symphony of flora, joy repels.

Harmonies of the Garden's Heart

In the garden, giggles bloom,
Silly flowers clear the gloom.
Bees dance in their bowler hats,
Chasing after cheeky cats.

The daisies wear polka dots,
While tulips tie their knotted knots.
Laughter fits within each petal,
Jokes that make the storks all meddle.

A sunflower sings a tune,
Underneath the glowing moon.
Worms play hide and seek so sly,
While crickets dance and whirl up high.

With every sprout and every bud,
A playful world springs from the mud.
In this patch of life's delight,
The blooms make every moment bright.

Kaleidoscope of Colors

A rainbow tumbles in the dirt,
Each color chuckles with a flirt.
Red and blue are friends today,
Making green, then running away.

Yellow daffodils tell jokes,
As purple pansies turn to blokes.
Orange blooms twist in delight,
Spreading cheer from morn till night.

Petals whirl in laughter's spree,
As petals dance, oh what a glee!
In this garden's lively play,
Colors wink and frolic, yay!

All these hues in joyful cheer,
Shake their leaves, they have no fear.
Together spinning wild and free,
In kaleidoscopes of memory.

Petal Rhapsody

In petals soft as cotton candy,
The blooms all grin, they look so dandy.
Silly ants march in a line,
Each one thinks it's doing fine.

The wind blows whispers sweet and light,
Tickling stems till they take flight.
Butterflies dressed up in styles,
Waltz around wearing big smiles.

A flower's joke, a daffy pun,
Brings laughter 'neath the shining sun.
While ladybugs swap funny tales,
As petals float like tiny sails.

In this rhapsody of delight,
Each blossom sparkles day and night.
When flowers wink and grasses sway,
It's laughter's bloom that leads the way.

The Verse of Each Blossom

Every flower tells a tale,
Of silly winds that make them sail.
Cactus jokes and ferns that sigh,
Join the laughter in the sky.

Rosebud whispers secrets low,
To daisies dancing down below.
They giggle loud, a raucous crew,
Creating laughter, fresh as dew.

Sunflowers wave their golden heads,
Swapping stories in their beds.
While violets tease the passing breeze,
In this garden, joy's the key.

So take a stroll among the cheer,
In blooms and laughter, have no fear.
Every petal, every sprout,
Will sing a tune we can't live without.

Gentle Fragrance of Longing

In a field of blooms so bright,
A bee trips, oh what a sight!
He lands on petals, soft and round,
Buzzing loudly, no grace found.

A squirrel sneaks a tiny treat,
While dancers shuffle on their feet.
The flowers giggle in the breeze,
As bees offer the clumsiest tease.

A butterfly with a funny sway,
Flutters by in a zany way.
The sun chuckles from up high,
As breezes whisper a playful sigh.

Amidst the laughter, joy does sing,
Cheerful blooms make hearts take wing.
In this garden, let's be free,
And dance along with glee, you see!

Dances of Delight

In the garden, colors clash,
Flowers twirl in a joyful bash.
A daffodil doodles, a snapdragon pranks,
While tulips give their colorful thanks.

Bees with hats buzz in a line,
Chasing shadows down the vine.
A rogue petal joins the fun,
As gales of laughter have begun.

Mushrooms sway to the tune of rain,
While ants march in a silly chain.
With each bloom, a chuckle grows,
In this party where humor flows.

Under the sun, they skip and play,
Bright blossoms have their humorous say.
Join the frolic, let spirits soar,
In this patch of joy, who could ask for more?

The Art of Quietude

In the stillness, a snail creeps slow,
With a tiny top hat, it's quite the show.
He tips his hat to the passing breeze,
Which rustles leaves with playful ease.

A frog on a lily, so plump and round,
Croaks out poems, a silly sound.
He pauses, winks, and takes a bow,
Nature's jesters playfully take their vow.

Ants march by in a busy trance,
While daisies giggle, their petals dance.
A silent beetle, with swagger so grand,
Pretends he's quite the ruler of the land.

So in this quiet, find the fun,
Where laughter flows just like the run.
With nature's charm and jokes to share,
The art of stillness has its flair.

Reflecting in Nature's Mirror

Puddles shimmer under the sun,
A frog jumps in—what a splash, what fun!
He catches his face, a silly sight,
Ribbiting jokes, all day and night.

The wind whispers tales of missed flights,
While trees throw shadows that dance with fright.
A feather floats down with a grin,
Tickled by laughter that lies within.

A curious cat sits, tail twitching high,
Watching the world with a sly little eye.
Mirrored in water, reflections sway,
Friendships bloom in the silliest way.

So let's skip stones, let worries fade,
In nature's embrace, the fun is made.
In each ripple, joy can be found,
As laughter rings all around!

Inked Blossoms

In a garden where giggles roam,
Flowers wear hats, so they feel at home.
The daisies debate over who's the queen,
While sunflowers pose, all tall and keen.

A tulip spills juice, the ants start to dance,
They hold a parade, oh what a chance!
The roses can't bloom for laughing too loud,
Their petals are red but they're feeling quite proud.

The bees play tag amidst the green,
Dodging each other, they're quite the scene.
In this bouquet of joy and cheer,
Nature scribbles its laughter here.

So when you wander through blooms so bright,
Listen for giggles, it's pure delight.
For in this patch where the colors clash,
Joy is the ink, and life's quite the splash!

Fables from the Flowerbed

In the flowerbed, secrets bloom,
With gossips shared under the moon.
A daffodil tells stories tall,
While ferns just giggle, standing small.

The violets wear fables like a crown,
Spinning tales that turn upside down.
Tulips with glasses read books of yore,
And daisies pretend to be a folklore.

There's chatter of petals in the breeze,
Making everyone laugh with ease.
The roses bet on whom will sprout,
The sunflower chimes in with a shout!

In this garden of whimsical lore,
You'll laugh and love and always want more.
For each blossom holds a tale to share,
In a world where giggles are everywhere!

Echoes of the Violet

A violet whispers, "Have you heard?
About the bee who lost his nerd?"
The daisies giggle and wiggle with glee,
While bumblebees buzz with a raucous decree.

They plotted a prank on the poor old rose,
Said he smelled like last week's garden hose!
The peonies blushed, trying not to chime,
But soon they joined in with perfect rhyme.

With laughter that tickles the soft spring air,
They dance in the sun without a care.
A garden party beneath the trees,
With sweet rhapsodies carried by the breeze.

In the echo of petals, joy takes flight,
The flowerbed brims with pure delight.
So if you stroll where nature's bright,
Listen for laughter, it feels just right!

Scribbled Petals

Scribbled petals with notes of cheer,
Whispers of joy float near and dear.
A bee's got a crush on a blooming rose,
While butterflies chuckle at their own prose.

Tulips are trading their colorful schemes,
Over who has the wildest of dreams.
The orchids snicker as a snail slips,
"Next time, dear friend, choose sharper trips!"

Pansies are plotting a grand masquerade,
With costumes of leaves in a colorful shade.
The garden blooms with reports of fun,
Where humor and petals forever run.

So join in the laughter, it's blooming bright,
In a world where all giggles take flight.
With each scribbled petal that's lost in the air,
The garden still whispers, "Life's never a bore!"

Storyteller Among the Blooms

In a garden where laughter sways,
Petals gossip of sunny days.
Bees wear hats, oh what a sight!
Telling tales from morn till night.

Butterflies dance with a flourish,
Tickling flowers, oh how they nourish.
While ants debate a crumbly feast,
A picnic for the tiniest beast.

A daisy cracks a silly joke,
As tulips giggle, nearly choke.
With daisies blushing in bright hues,
Our garden jesters paint the views.

Fragments of Fragrance

In this patch where scents collide,
Cabbage roses take a ride.
Mint shares laughter with the thyme,
Claiming it's always dinner time.

Lavender whispers quirky rhymes,
While sunflowers switch to sunny climes.
Fruity peels casually tease,
As marigolds sway with the breeze.

Jasmine sets the world aglow,
Bringing tales of tall and low.
Each bloom with quirks, each sprout so proud,
In this fragrant laughter, we're all allowed.

Vignettes in Violet

In the depths of purple hues,
Mirthful blooms invent the news.
Sweet violets share such silly dreams,
Plotting schemes with daffodil teams.

An iris tickles a bumblebee,
As petals chant in harmony.
Bubblegum bursts from laughing buds,
Sipping dew through flower floods.

A violet's voice, can you imagine?
Chasing woes away with magic!
In this realm of floral magic,
Every giggle feels so tragic.

Poetry of the Silent Garden

In the hush where wild things play,
Whispers rise and gracefully sway.
Snapdragons grin with toothy flair,
As peonies shake out their hair.

Tulips hold a secret feast,
Where cheeky bees become the least.
Floral puppeteers pull the strings,
While ladybugs flaunt their tiny wings.

In this garden, silence sings,
Crickets hop on secret swings.
Every leaf a chapter bright,
In the night's soft fluttering light.

Fables of the Softest Hues

In a land where petals chat,
A violet whispered to a hat.
"Why do you sit, so stiff and proud?"
"Because I'm waiting for a cloud!"

Each bloom has tales, oh what a sight,
Daisies dance in morning light.
Roses giggle at the bees,
While tulips sway in friendly tease.

In this garden full of cheer,
Every plant has a story near.
From silly seeds to leaves that wink,
Watch the flowers share and blink!

So gather 'round, don't be shy,
Listen close, let laughter fly.
For in this patch of joy and glee,
The softest hues will set you free!

Tangled in Floral Melodies

A daffodil strummed on a stem,
Playing tunes, oh what a gem!
Petunias clapped with spark and cheer,
While lilies laughed, their voices clear.

Mirthful songs in morning bliss,
A cheerful bug joins in the list.
Their voices soared, a melody,
Twirling petals, oh so free!

Caught up in rhythms, sweet and light,
Sunflowers swayed from left to right.
With every note, a chuckle burst,
As nectar-drunk bees sang first.

So let the blooms weave tales so bright,
In gardens where all hearts take flight.
For laughter spreads, like pollen flies,
In floral notes beneath the skies!

The Garden's Endless Script

Upon a vine, a gourd did sketch,
A humorous tale, the finest fetch.
"Oh, if you think I'm just a fruit!"
"Then take a look; I dance in boots!"

Budding ideas with smiles in bloom,
Weaving giggles in every room.
Rubbing leaves with playful hands,
Joke-telling roots make silly plans.

Each plot unfolds a quirky scene,
From flower crowns to frogs unseen.
Sun-kissed jokes on every leaf,
A garden of joyful disbelief!

So read the lines in shades of green,
Where flowers whisper, life's a screen.
With every breeze, a chuckle hops,
In this realm where laughter never stops!

Ink and Fragrance

In a fragrant jar, there lies a pen,
With petals' ink, oh where to begin!
A quirky quill both soft and sweet,
Writes stories that tickle your feet!

With every drop, a tale unfolds,
Of bees that barter with marigolds.
"I'll trade you sweetness, you give me flight!"
While daisies argue, "That's not polite!"

So scribble down, make laughter flow,
In lavender valleys where the giggles grow.
Each bloom inspired by jest and grace,
Ink and fragrance leave a trace.

For in this garden, heart and laugh,
We write our joy, a floral craft.
So grab your pen and join the spree,
In every whiff, life's a comedy!

Dreams in Bloom

With petals bright, they sway and dance,
In gardens where the giggles prance.
A sprinkle of laughter in the air,
As blossoms tease with playful flair.

They whisper secrets, wild and sweet,
While bees tap-dance on tiny feet.
Each color splashes on the green,
A canvas where the joy is seen.

Little bumbles buzz with glee,
As flowers hold a tea party spree.
Cups of dew and crumbs of sun,
United in laughter, oh what fun!

In every petal, mischief sings,
A tapestry of silly things.
Let's jump through these dreams, chase the light,
In bloom we find the silly bright.

The Weight of Softness

In fluff and frill, where giggles form,
Each gentle hue becomes the norm.
A soft embrace, a wink of cheer,
The weight of softness dances near.

Look closely now, can you believe?
A fuzzy hat upon a leaf!
With every breeze, it starts to spin,
A fashion show for plants to win.

Tickled pink, the blossoms grin,
While daisies wink, and turkeys spin.
Who knew that whimsy could be so light,
In gardens hosting pure delight?

A rolling laugh in every breeze,
As petals play beneath the trees.
With each soft step, they twirl around,
In this light-hearted, giggling ground.

Stories Beneath the Soil

In darkness deep, where whispers hide,
Roots telling tales of joy and pride.
The earth a storyteller, so sly,
Beneath the surface, laughter's nigh.

Worms recite poems, squiggly and long,
About the flowers that hum a song.
With every wiggle, they share a jest,
In the quiet world, they laugh the best.

Moles gossip tales of garden fame,
While daisies blush at love, not shame.
If you dig deep, a chuckle's found,
In this hidden realm, joy knows no bound.

Each rumor's rich, each story grand,
In the soft embrace of loamy land.
Beneath our feet, a comedy thrives,
In soil where laughter truly derives.

Ballet of the Butterflies

A flutter here, a twirl so spry,
As colors leap beneath the sky.
Lace-winged dancers, a pirouette,
Forget your worries, don't you fret.

In the garden stage, they take their flight,
With every flap, they spread delight.
Wings painted bright, like candy spun,
Each dip and dive adds to the fun.

They chase the sun, a giggling crew,
In a breeze that swirls in shades of blue.
With every landing, they steal the show,
A fleeting magic in the flow.

So let's applaud this vibrant play,
Where butterflies dance and laughter sways.
In nature's theatre, joy unfolds,
A ballet where the heart beholds.

Serenade of the Pastels

In fields of color bright, they dance,
Each petal winks, a merry glance.
With hues like candy, sweet and bold,
They whisper secrets, tales retold.

A flower's giggle in the breeze,
Tickling ants with dandelion tease.
They wear their crowns of velvet flair,
Bees buzzing softly, a buzzing fair.

They sway and twirl, a floral jest,
Holding court like a fanciful fest.
With every bloom, their laughter spills,
A pastel symphony that thrills.

Oh, how they prance, the garden clowns,
In sunlit skirts, no heavy frowns.
Each blossom knows just how to play,
In the serenade of yesterday.

In the Company of Blossoms

In a gathering of blooms, so sweet,
The daisies chatter, oh what a treat!
Lilies lounge in their fancy attire,
While tulips gossip, never tire.

"This shade of pink is all the rage!"
Said one with flair, taking center stage.
Daffodils nod, with their sunny grin,
While violets pout, losing the win.

Amongst the petals, the tales unfold,
Of secret romances, both brave and bold.
With bees as scribes, they write the song,
Of flower friendships that last lifelong.

And as the moon begins to gleam,
The blossoms dream their fragrant dream.
A concert of colors, where laughter reigns,
In the company of blossoms, joy remains.

Garden of Hidden Stories

In this garden, whispers bloom,
With tales that dance and flowers fume.
A rose recites a love affair,
While lilacs sigh, threading the air.

Each petal here knows how to tease,
From morning dew to wandering breeze.
Hiding stories beneath their folds,
Every bloom a secret, quietly holds.

Sunflowers stretch, tall and proud,
Adopting poses, drawing a crowd.
With laughter echoing between the rows,
They spill the beans on all that grows.

A playful jest, a flower's plight,
In colors vivid, oh what a sight!
This garden laughs, with hearts so free,
Where hidden stories bloom in glee.

Through the Veins of Nature

Around the corner, a jolly spree,
As nature laughs, so wild and free.
With roots that tickle, and leaves that swing,
In every crevice, you'll find the zing.

The daisies dance as the wind complies,
Tickling the grass, while beetles rise.
With each sunny burst, their spirits soar,
And skip along like never before.

A ladybug's polka, a humble show,
With blossoms bobbing, putting on a glow.
Beneath the boughs, where the lilies jive,
In the veins of nature, all come alive.

Oh, the jokes they share, woven in green,
With petals' laughter, sound like a dream.
Through the veins, let the fun persist,
In a world of blooms, you can't resist.

The Dance of Flora's Ink

In a world where flowers write,
Giggles bloom under soft moonlight.
Pens made of petals, colors swirl,
With every stroke, the laughing twirl.

Bees waltz by, in polka dot shoes,
Spelling out jokes in morning dews.
Violets chuckle, daisies play tag,
While ink spills joy in a bright flag.

Their stories spill onto the grass,
As butterflies giggle, never a pass.
Blossoms whisper tales, oh so grand,
In a garden plot that's simply unplanned.

A sunbeam grins, the clouds start to nap,
While nature giggles in a soft, warm wrap.
With every line, creation delights,
A dance of blooms on joyful nights.

Remnants of Colorful Dreams

Lost in a garden of vibrant hues,
Where dandelions sing the evening blues.
Petals laugh as they flutter near,
Whispers of stories only they hear.

A whimsy tale of the pink marigold,
Whose jokes are silly and never old.
The sunflowers nod, cheeky and bright,
As crickets crack jokes beneath the starlight.

Dreams of violets, a carousel spin,
Where wild thoughts in colors begin.
With every laugh, a sprout takes flight,
In this garden of giggles, such pure delight.

A jester bee on a quest for fun,
Paints the world with a kiss from the sun.
And in the rustle of leaves we find,
The ridiculous brilliance of nature's mind.

The Narrative of the Dew-Kissed

Dewdrops gather tales on each leaf,
Whispering secrets, a comic relief.
On morning's stage, they glimmer and shine,
Telling old stories that feel so divine.

A rollicking tale of a clumsy snail,
Who tripped on a petal, a slippery trail.
Laughing lilies fill up the void,
As he spins in circles, utterly toyed.

The sun peeks in, a mischievous sprite,
Tickling the buds with golden light.
Even the thorns seem to chuckle and sway,
In this whimsical plot of a silly day.

Through every droplet, laughter flows,
In the tapestry woven where color glows.
The world wakes up with a giggle surprise,
As the dew-kissed tales raise their colorful cries.

The Blooming Librarian

In the library where blossoms conspire,
Every petal a book, every stem a fire.
A librarian with roots deep in the ground,
Spins tales of wonder, laughter unbound.

The roses debate on who's the best,
While daisies dive in for a quick jest.
In every aisle, a burst of cheer,
Where floral friends gather, year after year.

With wildflowers whispering stories so bold,
They share the last page of secrets untold.
The librarian chuckles and shakes with glee,
As butterflies flutter with a funny decree.

Each book is a blossom, colored delight,
Returning with giggles that sparkle and light.
In this blooming realm, with pages that dance,
They spin tales that make every heart prance.

The Palette of Stillness

In a garden where clowns paint,
Colors collide, as flowers faint.
With giggles sprouting wide and free,
A splash of whimsy, just wait and see.

The daisies wear hats, a sight so rare,
While roses argue about their hair.
A waltz with the bees in polka dots,
This canvas of laughter, a true jackpot.

The sun takes breaks, it winks, it sighs,
Tickling petals, oh how time flies!
Each brushstroke a chuckle, bright and bold,
In this garden of stillness, stories unfold.

So dance with the daisies, sway with the breeze,
In this palette of humor, do as you please.
For every flower knows, and so do we,
Laughter is the root of our jubilee!

Heartbeats in Bloom

In the heart of the garden, a party ensues,
With daisies and lilies, all donned in their hues.
A sunflower spins, the show-off of the night,
While tulips chuckle, oh what a delight!

The bees bring the music, a buzzing parade,
As violets jive, their worries allayed.
A daffodil trips on its own lovely stem,
Creating a giggle, a floral mayhem.

Each bloom's got a secret, a prank up its sleeve,
They giggle and whisper, oh, who would believe?
As the moonlight dances on petals so fine,
Heartbeats of laughter, all perfectly aligned.

So join in the revel, let the laughter loom,
In this garden of jest, every heart finds its room.
For in every flower, a joke lies in wait,
Just breathe in the fun, oh isn't it great?

Lyrical Gardens

In lyrical gardens, where giggles arise,
Plants tell their stories beneath sunny skies.
A quirky old fern offers puns with a flare,
While daisies in tutus pirouette through the air.

A lavender sings with a voice so sweet,
As marigolds greet you, their dance is a treat.
But beware of the cacti, with prickles galore,
They jest with their jabber, a floral uproar!

Wisteria whispers, its secrets unfold,
While playful petunias are bold and uncontrolled.
Each blossom a bard, with tales full of cheer,
A garden of laughter, come gather near.

So wade through the petals, in joy lose your way,
For every bloom knows how to brighten your day.
In lyrical gardens, where humor won't cease,
Every flower's a punchline, finding sweet peace!

Petals Under Moonlight

Petals pirouette softly, beneath the moon's glow,
Twinkling laughter lingers, above the night's show.
A mischievous marigold starts a giggle spree,
With the stars as its audience, how could it be?

Chrysanthemums chuckle, under their breath,
In whispers of humor, they dance 'til the death.
A ballooning dandelion floats through the night,
While pansies throw shade with a laugh, what a sight!

The moon grins down, a jester in white,
Poking fun at the garden, so lively, so bright.
Every shadow holds secrets, every breeze brings a jest,
Under moonlight's embrace, we forget all the rest.

So gather your laughter, let petals take flight,
In this whimsical garden, all is pure light.
Each blossom a joker, a thrill in the dark,
With petals a-flutter, we find our spark!

www.ingramcontent.com/pod-product-compliance
Lightning Source LLC
Chambersburg PA
CBHW071849160426
43209CB00003B/485